Island Road #1

WAY STATIONS

© 1989 by Henry Gould

ISBN 0-945926-17-0

Henry Gould

WAY STATIONS

AlephoeBooks - Providence

1989

special thanks to Peter Gale Nelson
and **paradigm press**

Halloween. The sun's already down.
Everywhere leaves are gathering,
Lightly rustling and shivering,
Their ruddy bloom already fading,
The sun's dry wine drunk to the dregs.

The neighborhood grows anonymous.
Soon the small ghosts will appear,
Flickering and half-transparent
Under the streetlights, costumed
For space travel, or the Middle Ages.

This is that ancient harvest night.
Harvest of time, harvest of souls.
Tonight the years are buried quietly
Under a shroud of old leaves, and I
Am a child too, standing at the door.

It is moonlight in the darkness,
And the heart finding after midnight;
It is a boat unmoored on the water,
And the current circling by itself.

It is tomorrow; it is a light word
Floating through an open door,
And the wind moving in the quiet,
Whispering over the land of the dead.

Bees dance above closed lips;
In the clear shadow of the oak
Wherever they turn their heads
They follow the bright pattern.

Quietly, by the granite cistern
Under a crowded canopy of reds,
In the cool wind a broken spoke
Sways whichever way it slips.

MIDWAY

To give back to the rain
What was announced on the rooftops
In whispers, at the end of May--
The rain, a drowsy origin
Cradled in the huge bronze
And silver of twisted beech.

Your sounding, not like laughter
On dry streets, nor an obituary
Reminiscence, give and take
Of battering wind--but slight
Drumming on rough graves, midway
From the obscure haze of a lamp.

THE LAMP

A slow wind blows through the night,
Carrying summer in puffs of sighs;
Far off there in the valley hollows
A yellow lamp swings to and fro.

Tree-bark, tree-limbs creaking,
The muffled sounds in the warm air,
And overhead thin clouds hurrying
Under a wheeling shroud of stars.

Day will impress our crafty cities
With silver and bronze, the filigree
Of spiderwebs, moldering iron,
The legible engraving of farewells.

Night, and heavy-hearted woodlands,
And the rustling of uncut grasses
In the children's books, a lamp
Throwing a wide circle in the wind.

THE LITTLE GATE

Wind moving in the myriad branches,
Intricate tower on tower of shimmering light;
Wind bending the heads of the dandelions,
Whispering here and there in the afternoon sun.

Across the road within a shady canopy,
Framed by an oak tree and the sloping wall
Of a wooden shed, an old picket fence gate
Built for children hides in its grotto.

I sit with my children in the sandbox,
A square pineboard cosmos brought to life
By water and the word, a desert made to bloom
With the curious names and places of the earth.

But I sit like grandfather gazing into space,
Buried in the ordinary things of summer--
This forgotten world; this brilliant, empty light
This wooden gate, so near and so hard to find.

Time now for the trees to shroud the earth
With their dark branches, time
When the wind dies down,
And over the still mirror
A faded voice is whispering.

Time again to climb into the old
Music-box in the forest,
And wind the iron spring--

It is letter by letter,
Line by line.

NOW AND ENGLAND

The wind for France
Blusters and laughs.
Green hills, gathered
And chaste, gleam
Over the humped sediment.

And bowmen will carry the day.
Silence an awkward garment
Among the clear circles,
At the lighted feast
Of modesty and honor.

Only, in the mild air,
To say goodby. Or there,
In grandmother's book,
Rapunzel, glancing down
From her strange tower.

Or stars over the sea.
Or tongues of fire.
A hearth-blaze. Fold
My hands, light the
Four corners of the bed.

SONG

Lights of a faraway airplane
Drifting slowly over a full moon,
And the stirring of the cicadas
Deciphering an old rune--

Like a tiny Southern Cross
Heading northward into silence,
A cold, clear, painful silver
Stabs the summer's kind expanse.

Down below we'll make peace,
Our words twining, our gait slow.
We'll go round Mirror Lake,
Where the soulful swans row.

But the sirens are wailing,
And a churring of shadows
Escorts the swift pacing
Of these rolling billows--

And only a steady heartbeat
Over the flowering grave of love
Can bear the fruit of dying
On such thorny blows from above.

The poet is monotonous, his head
resting on her empty sleeve,
his voice out of the mineshaft
muttering rumors of precious gems.

And stars shine in the black sky,
peacefully, released at last
from that deep unspoken gloom
by his aimless, undying lament.

EPITAPH

He set his hand to many
Treacherous decrees,
And made many enemies
Among nobles of good family.

Quarrels being the cement
Of state, after the blood-
Scrawl of a name is understood:
Honorable Gloucester, noble Kent.

Yet who will rise to condemn
This prince of liberty's decay?
With a mortal wound he lay
By the seashore, crying "Jerusalem!"

They are nobody's children,
and they walk with your airplanes,
they touch your shadows.

Nobody heeds them,
they were born on the west side
of the train, in a heavy rain.

They are your time.
Their eyes close on your flag.
They will take no names.

They are nobody's children.
God is the worm in their hearts,
They were born of the Virgin.

from a cave

Such a small voice,
I would not stop to hear;
The sun was going down, and
There were no houses near.

Such a strange voice,
Whispering out of the ground--
Familiar, though it seemed
Unearthly, utterly profound.

Such a sweet voice,
Twining my cavern ear;
A vine for water jars, when
All the wedding guests are here.

at noon

Orpheus sings alone,
His lyre left in the wind
Moaning in elliptical harmony.

Persephone sleeps, her head
Hidden in her arms, and shadows
Of clouds passing over her hair.

And John, in his prison, hears
Dance music in the rooms above,
And the sound of an axe on stone.

TWO BROTHERS

Feverish forehead, dizzy words--
A lying man lies down again
Like a lump in the nursery,
On summer's hillside breast.

It was you I was calling to
In the far-off light;
Your shade, and my echo,
Your hand, and my scribbling,

Like two brothers struggling,
One with a lamb, the elder
With an iron plow, two boys
Inside a tangled village fence.

A man lies down and listens,
Fettered under the fretful salt;
Dreaming of drawing out the thorn
With a rightful, fiery tribute.

But molten tongs, loud hammers,
My weary workshop, brother--
A shanty under the sturdy trees,
Their calm crowns leaning together.

WOODEN HORSE

I

My garden is dry;
The wilderness is near.
Upstairs in a cold room
The pen forces its way.

Leah, Leah, with you
I labored against the bridle--
Bit two decades
Out of your side, old shrew,

Old fond, old shadow.
We buried Rachel
Along with the ring,
And soon we'll fly too--

On the back of a steed
Rigid, gelded with anger,
Brazen with time,
Unable to breed.

II

Unable to breathe
In the burning city,
Dido stares out toward
The sails' dark wreath.

We are undone,
We are betrayed--
Take this cup from me
Father, cries the son;

And Psyche bends low
Among the whisperers,
Among swallows taken,
Among those who know.

In the shaggy forest
The ghost of Turnus,
And Pilate suckling
At the wolf breast.

CROSSROADS

This compost of whispers,
Wrapped in a thin shawl.
A glint of chrysoprase,
Anthems, memorials.

Only this
Common marigold,
Stubborn with the rank
Smell of a carven root;

Shying from the light
Only to be changed,
And to bear your glance
Alone, in lunar disgrace.

Oh crossroads, green
Hiding place, oaken
Crown of narrow blood
At the crossroads!

Over the yellow gold
Of the casket, the sun
Turns black, the iron
Axe hangs on high:

A veil of shame,
A red scarf on the stones,
A flower burning,
And Joshua's horn.

WAY STATIONS

The child honoring you in dreams,
Embrasure of innocence, tender shoots
Of early radiance--your figure
Landscape, unfamiliar town, scent
Of May lilacs along a worn road.

Not to be known yet,
Only a heavy cloud pregnant
With summer rain
(Iron mortality, rust
Of decline not yet to be);

Gathering up your skirts
You find your way, slow path
Beyond the jealous decorations,
Fever of scorn, offended pride,
Dry branches crackling--a bonfire.

The wind exhaled, this world
Sprawled--a spring disaster, flocks of embraces
In the garage, under the oil refineries
Hospitable sirens, waltzing on broken silver.

And night deepened around the temple,
A yellow-black wafer, crust for the swans;
And the wind circled the olives, a morning watch
All night by the Kedron, all day by Euphrates.

And we'll meet again by the wintry river
Where we swaddled the sun in a double wreath,
Cedar and lilac, tangled in a knot of beaten
Gold--sea-roses, breathing in Jerusalem.

Summer was ocean, a deep gift,
Incubation of Joshua, solstitial parakeet.
And earth was borne into heaven,
Vaulted into heaven on boats of reeds.

And this May light in the neighborhoods,
Where a flowering clematis mantles the porch
In curls of shade, is preparation--
Enjoins old bones to climb the coruscating tree.

OCEAN STATE

Here the waters gather along the shore.
They meet the land breathing in foam,
And roll the sleepy pebbles and shells
Back into long sand waves as before.

Our moon, casting her antique spells.
A motionless iris in the whale's eye
Of the sea, her unspeakable name
Sinks to the bottom of lonely wells.

Her low whispers frame the deserted dome.
Her light covers the circus floor.
And she lifts, with one nocturnal sigh,
The heaving swells in a silver comb.

Summer is breathing in a hazy spray
Of watery mist and windy water, the waves
Dance to a slow dance over my sleeping.

*

The trees rise in their mask of silence.
This paper word their last dry leaf, slips
Through the foaming air, crumbles to soil.

*

Dig your fingers into the ground. The root,
The wooden word, is Adam's trowel and tomb,
Gathering all to one great breathing crown.

THE DARK GARDEN

Vines tremble in the night
Around the house's wooden doors,
Rustling in the soft breeze, whispering.

Otherwise, not a sound. The high
Moon stands over the hurrying clouds,

Motionless in the central dark;

The wind tries everywhere for a resting
Place, vainly turning over leaves;

And someone stands there in the shadows
Looking out at the dry garden, listening
To vine-limbs creak in the night air.

IMPERIUM

The Roman guards
Cast lots for your clothing,
The way time and fortune
Throw bones for kings' crowns;
You left them the shreds
Of the Lord's farewell gift,
Awaiting the shroud and the
Spices of paralyzed women.

Your voice remains hidden
Beneath the black mirrors,
Diffracted, diffused by the
Cold bones, the cold bones.

SABBATH EVE

Between the parchment of an ending testament
And tongue-tied shadows crowded in a dream--
Between blind feelers urgent in the city
And useless talent lodged in bitter syllables--

Hanging, balanced on a grim little hill
Among thieves and huddled followers, the Word
Consents to dying in an empty theater--
To match the futile world with an empty tomb.

In a rough-hewn four-poster
The moody Puritan sleeps.
Down the steep dark stair,
Slowly, a poor wife creeps.

Under a heavy kitchen box
There's a crust of dry bread;
Strong hands undo the locks;
She goes out by the shed.

The old redhead dreams on,
Kindly dawn slowly rises--
He sees a fatherly sun,
Gleaming strawberry ices,

And a justified Rome--
While his wife, thinly wan,
Espousing dear freedom,
Succors an orphan swan.

infin che'l veltro verra

Aboard a swift Greyhound
Adrift in America,
One of the grateful dead
Plays a slow harmonica.

Sons honor your fathers
And heed their command--
It's a surplus contempt
That lays waste to the land.

Fathers honor your sons
And regard the heart's law--
For it's ease and corruption
That open Hell's maw.

And I'll sing the dark waters
And keep the long watch
Til that Greyhound swings home
Across old Devil's Notch.

                                             <u>in RI</u>

No one will blame me
on the whispering shore
for lingering so long
near your small rose island.

Bees' slow honey
is the measure of summer;
morning and sundown,
by that rose double-arch.

And my tongue's dark island
leaves a late russet shadow--
dry relic of the voyage,
our lips' broken compass.

APRIL

Sunday afternoon in the gray rain.
I see a shriveled old woman,
hunched under a black umbrella
held tight like a turtle shell:

slowly she makes her way,
with each step her body lurching
sideways--and she's singing!
her clear voice dancing before her.